MW00913814

How to Memorize Bible Verses

Bible Verses

The Fast and Easy Way to Memorizing Scripture

Second Edition

Kyle Buchanan & Dean Roller

All rights reserved, No part of this publication may be
reproduced in any form or by any means, including scanning,
photocopying or otherwise without prior written permission of
the copyright holder.
Copyright © 2013 Memory Worldwide Pty Ltd
ISBN: 1481977768
ISBN-13: 978-1481977760

To Rach and Lexy

CONTENTS

Also by Kyle Buchanan & Dean Roller

The Companion Guide to How to Memorize Bible Verses:
A List of Key Words and Substitute Images

Memorize Bible Verses:
Complete Memory Stories for 100 Popular Bible Verses

Memorize Bible Books:
Complete Memory Stories for the
66 Books of the Old and New Testaments

For more information about these titles and a *free* sample copy
of "Memorize Bible Verses", please visit
www.MemorizeBibleScripture.com

1 INTRODUCTION

When I was a child I spent a lot of time repeating Bible verses over and over, all in an attempt to memorize them. It was like throwing mud against a wall. If you throw enough mud, some of it is going to stick. Unfortunately, most of it simply slides off and falls to the ground, which is incredibly disheartening. Splat.

And that is the reason why so few of us memorize God's word, even though so many of us would like to carry it with us every day. Memorization is hard, repetitive work.

Or is it?

As I grew up I took it for granted that repetition and rote learning were the only way to force new information into my brain.

And then one day I saw an amazing demonstration of memory by someone who memorized a pack of playing cards in only a few minutes. And I wondered – how do they do that? Is it a God-given gift that they're born with, or is it a learnt skill, like reading or riding a bike?

After some research I discovered that it's a bit of both. We all have an amazing memory already, so it really is a God-given gift. However, hardly anyone knows how to capture the full potential of their existing ability. So we do need to learn that skill. And I should stress, you don't need to improve your memory – you just need to learn how to use it properly.

And that's what this book is going to teach you.

The techniques I learnt, and that you will too, have actually been around for thousands of years. I am still at a loss to explain why they aren't more commonly known and used. They're very easy to learn.

I've taken the basic method that all memory 'professionals' use and adapted it to help memorize Bible verses.

I should clarify that this book is intended to be a simple and practical 'How to…' book. The fact you're reading this means I don't need to convince you on the 'Why to…' of memorizing scripture.

So let me tell you what we are going to cover in "How to Memorize Bible Verses".

First, I'll let you in on the big secret of memorization. And then we'll get straight into using it. It's going to be that simple.

We will go step by step through the exact same process used to create the visual memory stories for www.MemorizeBibleScripture.com, and I'll use plenty of examples to explain everything.

Once you're comfortable with the method for memorizing the actual verses, I'll explain how to embed the book, chapter and verse reference in your memory too. You will even be able to use the reference as a prompt to recall the verse itself. It sounds too good to be true, right?

To finish, we'll put it all together in one smooth process; touch on the optimal amount of revision (yes, even with this amazing method you'll need to do a little bit of revision to keep the memories there); and take a brief look at some other memory techniques you could play around with to memorize God's word.

Enough talk – let's get into the good stuff!

2 WHAT IS THE SECRET TO MEMORIZATION?

The great 'secret' to memorization is visualizing what you're attempting to remember.

This is common sense when you think about it. Do you remember the house you grew up in? What about your favorite teacher at high school?

As soon as you try to recall those things, you recreate an image of them in your mind. A visual image, because that's the way your memory works. And it didn't take any effort at all, right?

If your memory recalls pieces of information as an image, it makes sense that when you want to put new information into your memory, it would be best if that was in a visual form too. Image in, image out.

This is what your memory does naturally, without you even thinking about it. For example, try and recall what you have done today or yesterday from the moment you woke up. Even if you can't get every detail, there are hundreds or even thousands of details that you will remember, simply because you saw it all happen in front of you.

Why can you remember hundreds of new pieces of information about your day without even thinking about it, but you struggle to memorize a Bible verse of twenty words when you're trying really hard? It's because you're not on the same wavelength as your memory, you're speaking a different language. Your memory doesn't like rote learning and repetition, it likes to see things!

You didn't consciously try to memorize everything you did in the last day; your memory just soaked up the visual images. And when you recalled what you did it was like watching a little movie in your mind.

How amazing is the human memory?

Of course, your other senses will strengthen those images too, when you smell, taste, hear or feel something, but for most of us, our memory is predominantly visual.

And the cool thing is your mind doesn't differentiate between an image you physically see with your eyes or one you see vividly with your imagination. Your memory will grab onto both types of picture.

The goal then, is to *consciously* use your memory in the same way that you normally use it *unconsciously*.

This sounds ridiculously simple but when you give it a bit more thought you realize that it can't be so easy.

Can it?

When I was a student at high school and college, I was told by various teachers and lecturers that visualizing things in your mind is the key to memory. Unfortunately, that was all I was ever told – nobody ever explained how to do that in a useful way.

It's easy enough to create a mental image of physical objects you know, but how does that help when you're trying to memorize a quote from Shakespeare, or a list of steps to create a successful marketing plan? How do you picture something intangible?

That is the first step in memorizing Bible verses. You'll learn how to turn intangible words on a page into something tangible you can visualize in your mind, and allow your memory to grab onto. That's the first major step.

After visualization, the second important technique memory experts use is association.

Think again about everything you've done today or yesterday after you woke up. The countless details that you can see in your mind demonstrate the power of visualization.

But how do you remember the sequence of them all correctly? That's the power of association. It's like a relay race where the baton is passed from one runner to the next.

After I woke up this morning and used the bathroom, I was eating cereal and watching some morning TV. I laughed so hard at something the weatherman said during the weather forecast that I spilt my mouthful of cereal on my clean business shirt. Because of that I recall having to change shirts and putting on my favorite pink shirt, even though it's not Wednesday (don't ask). My pink shirt always makes me feel good about the world, and on the bus to work my friend commented on my cheerful mood.

Beginning with the simple image of my spilt cereal, I'm easily able to recall the order of a number of other events during the day because of the associated links. I went from the cereal to my pink shirt to the details of the conversation with my friend on the bus.

Remembering the correct sequence is very important when we try to memorize a Bible verse. If we remember all the words in a Bible verse but not the order they go in, we'll have verbal alphabet soup.

You've probably heard of professional downhill skiers or bobsled drivers practicing by visualizing the race course from the starting gate to the finish line. That's an example of using both visualization and association. They visualize every turn and straight and associate it with what they will need to be doing at that moment, and what is going to happen on the next part of the course.

The chances are that neither you nor I are going to be professional athletes (speak for yourself, I hear you say) or competitive memory athletes, but we can still use those same techniques of visualization and association to help us memorize verses of scripture.

We will begin by deciding which key words in a single verse we really need to memorize. Then the goal will be to substitute those key words with images that can be easily pictured in your mind. Would the word 'admirable' be easier to remember if you pictured a bull dressed as an admiral – Admiral Bull?

That's the visualization part.

Then we'll focus on associating each of those key word images with the image that follows. And we'll do that by creating some silly and ridiculous stories that your memory will retain more easily.

And that's the association part.

My morning wouldn't have been as easy to remember if I'd kept my cereal in my mouth and worn a bland white shirt to work. So together, we'll envision stories where we spray breakfast cereal everywhere and wear rainbow colored bikinis.

It might not be pretty but it's going to be memorable.

Finally, I should clarify that these mental imagery memory techniques are not new. They're the basis of 'mnemonic' memory methods that have been used since the time of Ancient Greece. For the last 50 years they have been the subject of academic research around the world – often in the fields of educational and cognitive psychology – which has proven their effectiveness. If you'd like a free research report which summarizes those scientific studies, please visit our website at www.MemorizeBibleScripture.com

The evidence shows that mental imagery methods are more effective than repetition in moving new information to your *long term memory*. This is what makes them 'fast'.

The average person might be able to use repetition to memorize a Bible verse within about five minutes, but it is only in their *short term memory*. The typical result of that approach means the verse is forgotten within a couple of days. It takes the brute force of continuous repetition and rote learning to successfully get the information into your long term memory. That's the part that is slow and no fun.

As you'll see, while visual memory mnemonic methods typically take more effort initially, they are quicker in transferring information to your *long term memory*. That means overall, these techniques are faster and more effective. And that's our goal.

Like most proven memory systems, the method used in this book relies on silly and ridiculous images and/or stories. This shouldn't be mistaken for intentional irreverence to the Lord's word – it's simply the most effective way for you to memorize scripture.

However you learn the Lord's word, we hope you know how wonderful your God-given memory truly is.

3 CHOOSING THE KEY WORDS TO MEMORIZE

Let's talk about precisely what we're going to memorize.

If you wanted to remember the phrase "The Son of God", and you were given:

"___ Son ___ God",

you'd undoubtedly be able to figure out the remaining words are 'The' and 'of'.

When we look at any sentence there are *key words* which carry the foundation meaning of what's being communicated, and then there are *filler words* which really just link together the key words.

In the example above, the key words are 'Son' and 'God' and the filler words are 'The' and 'of'.

Since we can figure out the filler words without having specifically memorized them, it makes sense that we won't make extra work for ourselves by trying to remember every single word. Being able to recall the key words or phrases will be sufficient.

As you progress through this book you'll start to realize that there's a balance between how much of a verse you want to memorize word for word, and how much work it'll take to memorize it.

You can definitely aim to use these techniques for every single word, but it will take more effort to achieve that goal.

For that reason I recommend aiming to memorize only the key words. Naturally, the next question to ask is how many words to designate as key words. In the end it will come down to your personal preference.

For the book "*Memorize Bible Verses: Complete Memory Stories for 100 Popular Bible Verses*", we attempted to include as many words as possible. That meant at least half of the words in every verse were memorized. Adding the remaining filler words to complete the verse is simple to do, even if a small amount of practice is required.

Let's go through an example.

> John 4:1 says "Now Jesus learned that the Pharisees had heard that he was gaining and baptizing more disciples than John".

> What are the key words that convey the meaning of this verse? And which words don't really add any extra meaning?

If you saw:

"___ Jesus learned ____ ___ Pharisees ___ heard ____ __ ___ gaining ___ baptizing ____ disciples ____ John",

I think you could get a pretty good grasp of what the verse is saying. And that's not even using half the words in the verse.

Now see if you can complete the filler words without looking at the full verse. It's pretty easy to do.

As you learn the methods in this book you will decide for yourself how many key words to use and memorize, and which ones they are.

Nouns like 'Pharisees' and 'disciples' typically make the best key words. Verbs like 'heard' and 'baptizing' can be slightly more challenging but are also good to use. Definite and indefinite articles like 'the' and 'a' are at the opposite end of the usefulness scale. It's best to leave those as filler words. (Yes, I had to Google what 'definite and indefinite articles' are too – let's just call them 'words').

As we go through the next chapter on substituting words for images, you'll develop a better understanding of why some words are better key words than others. For the moment, just select words that you think help convey the sentiment of the verse.

We'll look at Matthew 6:33 as another example, before we move on.

"But seek first his kingdom and his righteousness, and all these things will be given to you as well."

Select what you think are the key words that provide the essence of the verse, and you'll get something like:

"___ seek first ___ kingdom ___ ___ righteousness, ___ all _____ things will __ given __ you __ ____."

As you practice the complete memorization method you'll figure out for yourself pretty quickly whether you need to include more or less key words.

Now let's move on to turning these key words into images that we can easily visualize in our head.

4 HOW DO YOU SUBSTITUTE WORDS FOR IMAGES?

Having selected the words we want to memorize, we need to be able to picture them clearly in our mind. How do you turn a word on a page into a picture that you can vividly imagine?

Sometimes it's easy. When I read the name 'Jesus', I automatically picture a man with long dark hair and beard and flowing white robes.

Sometimes you need to get a little creative. The word 'believes' doesn't represent a physical object that you can visualize. What if you picture leaves that are yellow and black and make a loud buzzing noise? 'Bee leaves' remind you instantly of the word 'believes'.

As you can see, the challenge in substituting mental images for words is that sometimes the literal meaning of the word is not a tangible object. We need to turn something intangible into something tangible that we can picture and will remind us of the original word.

You can probably see where we're headed, so I'll lay out

some suggested guidelines and then we can go through them one by one.

- You need to get creative
- Think about the literal meaning of the word
- Consider the pronunciation of the word
- Check if the way the word looks on the page reminds you of other words
- Perhaps the word could be symbolized by an image of something else
- Could you break the word into parts to create other words?
- Adding words or letters to create another word may help
- A phrase may be easier to visualize than a single word
- Create your own visual vocabulary

You need to get creative

Images need to stand out in your mind. This is an overarching principle to keep in mind during this chapter and the next, when we start to create stories out of our images.

We don't easily remember everyday pictures. I saw hundreds of people on my way to work today, but I don't recall many of them, because they all looked completely normal. However, if one of them had been wearing a chicken suit, I would have remembered her.

You have to give your memory something to latch onto.

How would you picture the disciples? An image of twelve men might seem ok now, but your memory will soon water that image down, and you'll only recall them as a group of men of an unknown number. How will you remember that they're the disciples and not a group of friends on the way to Burger King?

We need to associate in our mind that there are twelve men, so what else comes in groups of twelve? A jury in a court trial has twelve people. There are twelve months in the year. Eggs come in a carton of twelve.

If we go with the egg idea, we could imagine that there are twelve tiny men who live in an egg carton. Or they could be normal sized men who drive around in a bus which is a giant egg carton with wheels. What if we had a carton of real eggs which were each dressed up as a man with a beard and long hair drawn on it, and a flowing robe belted around the middle?

Yes, these are very silly images, but you'll see that the next time you hear the disciples mentioned, a mental picture of eggs will instantly come into your head. Your memory latches onto creative images that stand out.

Think about the literal meaning of the word

The easiest place to start is to check if the meaning of your key word is something tangible that we can picture straight away. Is the key word a noun, verb, adjective or other type of word? If it's a noun, our job is usually quite simple.

Matthew 16:18 contains the word 'rock'. This is a word that creates a mental picture automatically. We could imagine a dark grey rock the size of a baseball, but there's plenty of opportunity here to be more creative.

Picture a rock the size of a car that can sing. It has facial features including eyes and a mouth, and it loves to sing rock and roll songs. It's a rockin' rock.

Nouns aren't always easy to picture though.

Jeremiah 29:11 mentions the word 'plans'. "'For I know the plans I have for you', declares the Lord…" In this context it refers to intentions, which isn't easy to visualize.

However, the word 'plans' can also be used in reference to drawing plans or building plans. An enormous piece of paper with architectural drawings on it would be simple to picture, and would still give us our key word.

How about verbs or 'action words'?

The word 'fall' is mentioned in Romans 3:23. By itself this is a difficult word to picture, but as soon as we think about how an object might fall, it becomes far simpler. This relates to substituting phrases rather than single words, and also how we join the individual images using a story (covered in the next chapter).

Adjectives or 'descriptive words' will also usually need to be related to another image.

In Acts 17:11 are the words 'noble character'. The adjective 'noble' refers to being king-like, so we could either envisage a king by himself, or we could link it with the word 'character' and think about a cartoon character wearing a king's crown.

Consider the pronunciation of the word

I truly admire anyone who learns English as a second language – it must be so confusing. Two words with different spelling and meanings can be pronounced in exactly the same way. That plays right into our hands.

Take the words 'need', 'be' or 'but'. None of them provide an automatic mental picture for us. How about the words 'kneed', 'bee' or 'butt'? Suddenly we've struck gold!

Someone being kneed in the belly is a strong visual. A bee is very easy to picture, especially if we get creative and make it the size of a watermelon. And it's very easy to imagine the sight (and feeling) of falling on your butt.

What about similar pronunciations? When I'm struggling to think of a substitute picture for a key word, I check if there's another word or phrase that sounds similar and provides a stronger mental image.

For example 'other' becomes 'udder'; 'condemnation' becomes 'condiments'; and 'Immanuel' becomes 'eye manual'.

Check if the way the word looks on the page reminds you of other words

Since each of our brains work in their own unique way, you might look at a word on a page and be reminded of another word or phrase, especially if you ignore the correct pronunciation of your key word.

With apologies to anyone named Timothy, whenever I see that name I always think of 'tie moth'. And I visualize a moth the size of an eagle, wearing a necktie.

In the same way, when I see the word 'finally' I picture an alleyway filled with fins, as if sharks were swimming around in the concrete – 'fin alley'.

Perhaps the word could be symbolized by an image of something else

Symbolism is a great way to create a mental image that immediately links in your mind to the key word. 'Peace', 'life' and 'love' are very common words, but they're not easy to visualize.

A peace symbol would obviously make you think of the word 'peace'; a new born chick crawling out of its shell could represent 'life'; and love hearts are the symbol that everyone immediately associates with 'love'.

Could you break the word into parts to create other words?

One technique I really like is thinking about how the word is pronounced and seeing if it's actually a couple of other unrelated words that can be pulled apart.

We saw previously how 'believes' becomes 'bee leaves'. From a difficult word to picture we've gone to two nouns that form a creative image together.

In the same way, 'require' could become 'reek choir' and we'd picture members of a choir who can't stand the smell of each other. Perhaps they're covered in sweat, rotting food and any other gross ideas you have.

'Bearing' is a challenging word to find a substitute image for, until you turn it into 'bear ring'. Either a large gold ring with a statue of a fierce looking bear on it, or a bear wearing a large diamond ring from Tiffany's would be memorable pictures.

A phrase may be easier to visualize than a single word

There are a couple of great benefits to visualizing a phrase rather than just a single word. Firstly, it can help you out if you're faced with a challenging word. Secondly, it reduces the number of images that your memory needs to grab onto. Simplest is best.

As an example, we'll take the phrase '...enter the kingdom of God...' from John 3:5.

If we were using single key words we'd probably take 'enter', 'kingdom' and 'God', create three separate images and then have to link them together with a story.

Instead, we could use a single image of a figure walking up a hill and entering a huge castle which has a figure of God (represented by an old, white haired man in flowing robes) standing on one of the highest parapets, looking out at his kingdom.

Create your own visual vocabulary

Once you've found a good substitute image for a particular word, don't reinvent the wheel.

When we were creating the stories for "Memorize Bible Verses", we made a vocabulary list. It had all of the key words on one side, and all of the related visual images on the other side.

As each new verse was started, it was simple to refer to the list and check if there was already a substitute image for a particular key word. The more verses you do, the larger the vocabulary list becomes and the easier it gets. We currently have a list of around 600 images to refer to.

If you are looking for a shortcut to creating your own visual memory stories, we have published our 'visual vocabulary' as "*The Companion Guide to How to Memorize Bible Verses: A List of Key Words and Substitute Images*". It provides the image and explains how the substitution was created between the word and mental picture.

Now that you know how to translate words into images, we can start to link them all together. During the next chapter I'll talk about creating stories that will lock your chosen verse into your memory. And we'll also re-visit our substitute images and what we can do to bring those pictures to life even more.

5 USING STORIES TO LINK IMAGES

It's time to write some crazy stories. This is how we will use the second secret weapon of memory experts – association.

Each of our key words now has a related mental image, but they're all a jumble with no particular order. It's like a big steaming bowl of alphabet soup.

To sequence our words correctly we'll create a mental movie that you'll be able to watch in your mind. That will allow you to associate each image with the one that follows, giving you a Bible verse rather than verbal alphabet soup.

I'll give you an example first, and then we'll go through some general rules that will help you unlock your inner Salvador Dali (if you've ever seen paintings that looked like they were the dream of an unbalanced mind who'd taken some crazy pills and hit his head, they were probably by Dali - on one of his more normal days).

Let's look at Ephesians 4:11. The key words I've chosen to memorize are in bold. This is a challenging verse to correctly memorize in order due to the list of people it mentions.

"**So Christ himself gave** the **apostles**, the **prophets**, the **evangelists**, the **pastors** and **teachers** …"

And my substitute images are below:

Key word	Substitute image
So	sew
Christ	Christ on the cross
himself	hymn self
gave	gave (action)
apostles	twelve eggs painted like the apostles
prophets	graph of profits
evangelists	Linda Evangelista
pastors	pastas
teachers	teachers in class rooms

Here is my story to link together all of those images. Be sure to picture everything clearly in your mind.

Imagine that you are trying to sew up a hole in your jeans, which is currently revealing your bottom. The sewing needle you're using is the size of a baseball bat and the thread is like bright orange string. You end up with some very bright and untidy stitch work. Sew = So.

The stitching looks less than desirable, so you decide to cover it up with a fabric patch of Christ on the cross. Christ is wearing a crown of thorns and is bleeding, and once the patch is on, the blood from the picture starts to drip onto your jeans. Bright red drops of blood on the blue denim. Christ on the cross = Christ.

Then the picture of Christ comes to life, and he begins to sing a hymn about himself. For a picture so small you'd expect a soft, high pitched voice, but this is a deep baritone and extremely loud. The picture is quite animated as he sings the hymn about himself. Hymn self = himself.

In the middle of his hymn, the animated picture's stomach starts to rumble, almost drowning out his loud singing. So he stops and pulls from his pocket a carton of twelve eggs. Each of the twelve eggs has a face painted on it and is dressed in tiny robes. The animated picture of Christ carefully chooses an egg and then gives you the rest of the carton. He gave them to you. Gave twelve eggs painted and dressed like the apostles = gave apostles.

You hold the carton of eggs in your hands and watch the remaining egg apostles all huddle together discussing something. Then they hoist up a big chart showing a graph of profits getting bigger and bigger, and the graph doesn't show a line but a picture of a pile of money getting larger and larger. Profits = prophets.

You watch the pile of profit on the graph getting higher and higher, and then suddenly the chart is ripped from the hands of the egg apostles by Linda Evangelista. Linda Evangelista is a former supermodel (if you can't picture her clearly, Google her image or just picture a beautiful woman and name her Linda Evangelista). Evangelista = evangelists.

Linda Evangelista takes the chart, tears it into tiny pieces, and adds it to some assorted pastas that she's cooking, as if it were seasoning. There's spaghetti, rigatoni and penne, and she drops the torn profit chart into each of them. No doubt the profits will make the pastas very rich (I apologize, I couldn't resist). Pastas = pastors.

Once she's happy with how the pastas are cooked, Linda Evangelista spoons them into buckets and gives them to teachers in their class rooms. She walks around, interrupting teachers in the middle of lessons to give them a bucket of pasta. Linda Evangelista is in such a hurry that she throws the pasta buckets at some teachers, and they get covered in pasta and rich sauce. Teachers = teachers.

After reading this story you'll be able to watch it like a movie in your mind. You are sewing your jeans (So) and stick on a fabric patch of Christ on the cross (Christ), who began to sing a hymn about himself (himself) and then gave you some egg apostles (gave apostles). The egg apostles showed you a chart of profits (prophets) before it was snatched away by Linda Evangelista (evangelists) who added it to some buckets of pasta (pastors) which she handed out to teachers (teachers).

Add the remaining filler words and you have Ephesians 4:11.

"So Christ himself gave the apostles, the prophets, the evangelists, the pastors and teachers …"

Now that you've seen what we are aiming to achieve, we'll introduce some general guidelines.

- Exaggerate each individual image
- Appeal to all of your senses
- Make the story and images dynamic
- Swap images around
- Create ridiculous or silly images
- Sequence is important

Let's go through each of these briefly.

Exaggerate each individual image

Each image will be more memorable if it stands out. Embellish the size and number of images wherever possible.

A normal sized sewing needle is not particularly memorable. One the size of a baseball bat stands out in your mind. And the effort of picturing something so unusual helps you concentrate on that image and makes it stick in your mind.

Increasing the size of something to gargantuan proportions is typically better than reducing its size.

Likewise, increasing the number of an image works better than reducing it. Picturing Linda Evangelista making thousands of buckets of pasta and seeing her amidst a sea of pasta would be better than having her cook one bucket of each type of pasta.

Exaggerate and embellish wherever possible. The goal is to *not* be plausible. Plausible is not memorable.

Appeal to all of your senses

While your memory is predominantly visual, if you make a story a full sensory experience it will be far more effective.

Make colors stand out, like bright red blood on blue denim. It would have been even more effective if it had been bright green blood. Use unexpected and garish colors.

Appeal to your senses of smell, sound, touch and taste wherever possible.

What did Linda Evangelista's rich pasta smell and taste like? Did the egg apostles smell of anything? How heavy were they in your hands? If they'd been as heavy as gold you could have imagined yourself struggling to hold them. They might have smelled of rotten eggs too. That would have stuck in your nose and mind.

Were you able to imagine the sound of the singing from the fabric picture of Christ? What would you usually expect to hear from a particular image? Try to make it unexpected.

Make the story and images dynamic

Pretend you're the director of this little mental movie that you're creating. Make it an action blockbuster.

Your memory is a demanding audience and it wants to be entertained. When you have an image that is typically inanimate, make it walk and talk. Like the fabric patch picture of Christ on the cross, make it sing and bleed if you can.

Can you make your pictures crash together? Or dance? Or be upside down or on top of each other?

Swap images around

An easy trick to use is to swap images around. The start of our story had you sewing with a large needle. It might have been even better if the large needle had been using you as a huge needle to sew.

If you needed to remember a chair, instead of picturing yourself sitting on the chair, the chair could sit on you.

Create ridiculous or silly images

There's a time and place for being conservative and sensible. Now is not that time. Engage your creative mind and challenge yourself to use increasingly ridiculous mental pictures.

The more silly, ridiculous or downright outrageous, the more effective your story will be.

Sequence is important

How you link each image is crucial to you remembering the story in the correct sequence. Wherever possible, make it like a relay baton being passed from one runner to the next.

The story for Ephesians 4:1 followed the story from the sewing to the patch of Christ on the cross, to the egg apostles and so on.

If you had sewn on a patch of Christ, then another patch of the egg apostles, then one of a profit graph, you wouldn't be able to recall the correct order of those images. You could have sewn on the patches in any order.

By creating a separate link between each picture, like a chain, you will have a logical progression through the story.

A good way to check if you've done this effectively is to see if you can recite the key words backwards. Start with the final image in the story and rewind through your mental movie. There is little practical benefit in being able to recite Bible verses backwards, but I suppose everyone needs a party trick.

6 HOW DO YOU MEMORIZE REFERENCES?

Can you believe you've already learnt how to memorize a Bible verse without resorting to the brute force and tedium of rote learning and repetition? This method is so much easier and a lot more fun. Your memory will thank you.

It's obviously important being able to reference what Bible verse you are quoting. You lose street cred when you quote a verse and then say "That's from the Bible ... somewhere".

The challenge of memorizing a book, chapter and verse reference is the same as dedicating a verse to memory. We need to create mental images of firstly the name of a book, and then of some numbers.

We'll use our substitution techniques for the names of various books of the Bible. Since we've already mastered that in the earlier chapter, I'll give some examples below but won't re-cover old ground.

What about those chapter and verse references? How do you visualize numbers?

The trick here is to have a fixed image that relates to each digit. There are various ways of doing that, but I think the simplest one to learn quickly is by using rhyming words.

I'll introduce our rhyming words/images first and then explain how we use them.

Number	Rhyming word/image
Zero	Hero
One	Gun
Two	Shoe
Three	Tree
Four	Door
Five	Jive
Six	Sticks
Seven	Heaven
Eight	Gate
Nine	Wine
Ten	Hen

In the world of memory experts, these words are called 'peg' words. When we hang a memory or number on each word, it's like hanging a jacket on a coat peg where we'll know to retrieve it later.

If you go down the list you'll see that each number has a word which rhymes with it. So if you picture a gun in your mind, you'll be able to figure out that it relates to the number one. No other number rhymes with gun. Likewise, if you picture a tree, it could only relate to three.

You'll be able to learn this list in a couple of minutes.

Make a clear mental picture of each image and then when you hear a number, the related image will pop into your head.

Let's look at an example so you can clearly see how to use this system. 'Romans 5:12' is an easy place to start.

First we need a substitute image to help remind us of the book of Romans. A Roman centurion or Roman soldier is pretty easy to visualize, so we'll use that.

To translate '5:12' into images, we substitute our rhyming words and it becomes 'jive, gun, shoe'.

Then our task is to join up our images of a Roman centurion, jive, gun and shoe using one of our crazy mental movies.

Picture a Roman centurion dressed in shiny armor with a mane of red horse hair sticking out the top of his helmet, and driving along in his chariot. Roman centurion = Romans.

He reaches down to the dashboard of the chariot and turns on his sound system, which begins pumping the song 'Rock Around the Clock'. While he's still driving along, the Roman starts to jive around to the music, twisting his hips and swinging his arms by himself. Jive = five.

As he's dancing away, he accidentally knocks the gun which he's wearing on his hip. Nobody told him that guns aren't meant to be invented for another thousand years. The gun is tucked into his belt and it's an enormous Magnum .44 hand gun, shiny silver and looks ferocious. When he knocks it with a flying arm it accidentally fires with a loud 'bang!' Gun = one.

The gun fires straight down and the bullet goes straight through the Roman's shoe. He takes his shoe off to inspect the damage. The shoe is actually a Nike basketball shoe, and there is now a large hole where his toes will stick out. Miraculously the bullet went straight through the shoe without touching his foot. Shoe = two.

When you watch your mental movie, you'll see the Roman driving along in his chariot (the book of Romans) when he turns on the music and starts to jive (chapter five). As he's dancing he hits his gun and it fires with a loud 'bang!' (verse 1...) The bullet makes a huge hole in his shoe (verse ...2).

It couldn't be any easier, you've just memorized the reference 'Romans 5:12'.

With some references it might seem difficult to know which number is the chapter and which is the verse. For example, for 'Romans 13:1' we would create a story using 'Roman centurion, gun, tree, and gun'. How do we know if the reference is 'Romans 1:31' or 'Romans 13:1'?

For that reason, use the rule that the verse number must always have two digits in it. Instead of 'Romans 13:1' we would use 'Romans 13:01' and we'd create a story around 'Roman centurion, gun, tree, hero and gun'.

The image I always use for 'hero' is a picture of Superman, a very famous super hero. That image allows for great creativity in your stories.

When we create a story to memorize an entire verse, we'd

naturally start with the verse reference. The reference story would then join up smoothly to the mental movie for the verse itself. We'll put it all together in the next chapter and you'll see how easily it all flows.

Once you have a complete visual story, the reference will actually prompt you to recall the verse itself. If someone asks you what Romans 5:12 says, you'd convert that reference into images. You'd watch your mental movie of that part of the story and it would flow into the story for the actual verse.

Instead of being an extra memory challenge, the verse reference becomes a memory aid. This is sounding easier and easier, isn't it?

Here are some examples of substitute images I've used for book names, just to help you on your way.

Book name	Substitute image
Acts	axe
Deuteronomy	judo mummy
Galatians	galoshes
Genesis	Jen's sis
Luke	Luke Skywalker
Philippians	(Prince) Philip

The next chapter will revise everything we've learnt so far, and go through some complete examples.

7 PUTTING IT ALL TOGETHER

Now that we've learnt each part of this simple method, let's put them all together so you can see how easily it works.

The steps to follow are:

1. Choose the key words from the verse we want to memorize
2. Replace the book, chapter and verse reference with substitute images
3. Replace each of the key words in the verse itself with substitute images
4. Create a visual story which links all of the images together

The first verse we'll use as an example is Proverbs 3:5, which says "Trust in the Lord with all your heart and lean not on your own understanding"

1. Choose the key words from the verse we want to memorize

The key words I've chosen to memorize are in bold below.

"Trust in the **Lord** with **all your heart** and **lean not** on your **own understanding"**

2. Replace the book, chapter and verse reference with substitute images

Following our rule to always have two digits in the verse reference, we add a zero and our reference becomes 'Proverbs 3:05'.

Reference	Substitute image
Proverbs	pro herbs
3 (three)	tree
0 (zero)	hero
5 (five)	jive

3. Replace each of the key words in the verse itself with substitute images

Key word	Substitute image
Trust	trussed
Lord	English Lord
all	awl
your heart	yore heart
lean not	lean knot
own	belongs to
understanding	standing under

4. Create a visual story which links all of the images together

There is a wonderful garden bed of herbs, filled with rosemary and thyme and basil, and they are such high quality herbs that they're pro herbs (professional herbs) and they have their own sponsorship deals and tiny sponsor's signs and logos on their leaves. Pro herbs = Proverbs.

Into the middle of this herb paradise suddenly crashes an enormous tree with a very wide trunk. It makes a very loud 'thud' as it lands, and the earth shakes beneath it. Herbs go flying everywhere. Tree = three.

Superman (our hero) flies down out of the sky and lifts up this huge tree and spins it around on his fingertips, despite its enormous size. Hero = zero.

Then Superman starts to dance with the tree, doing the jive. The tree isn't particularly limber, even if it is a bit of lumber. Jive = five.

'Pro herbs, tree, hero, jive' gives us 'Proverbs 3:05'.

In the middle of the jive, Superman suddenly throws the tree to the ground and ties it up with a long rope so it is trussed like a calf in a rodeo. Superman uses so much rope that by the time he's finished, the tree can barely be seen because of the rope. Trussed = trust.

The tree is lying on the ground all trussed up when an English Lord walks up to it, dressed in his long white wig and red cloak with white fur trim. The white wig is ridiculously long and curly, and reaches almost to the ground. He might look at home in the House of Lords in London, but he looks a bit silly. English Lord = Lord.

The English Lord pats the tree and looks at the ropes that are wrapped around it. He takes out an awl and uses it to untie the large knots that are in the rope. An awl is a leatherwork tool that looks like an icepick or a screwdriver with a sharp pointed end. Picture it as being the size of a baseball bat, which makes it look more like a weapon than a leatherwork tool. Awl = all.

It takes a while and the Lord has to be careful not to poke the tree with the awl, but eventually he manages to completely untie the tree. The tree is overcome with gratitude for being un-trussed by the Lord, and his heart bursts open with gratitude. The tree's chest opens up and his heart is completely visible, bright red and pumping wildly, but completely covered with cobwebs. The cobwebs show that the heart is extremely old, from the time of yore, so it's a yore heart. Yore heart = your heart.

The tree stands up, holding its heart in so it doesn't fall out, and leans over the Lord with a giant knot that is still tied in the rope. The knot is the size of a basketball. He leans right over with the knot and gently holds it above the head of the Lord. Lean knot = lean not.

Then the tree gives the knot to the Lord to make his own. The Lord admires his very own knot, and writes his name on it to make sure that everyone knows it's his own. He writes his name in fluorescent green ink. Owns the knot = own.

A wild storm suddenly erupts with rain, thunder and lightning, but the English Lord holds the giant knot up above his head. The knot starts to expand in size even further and completely shelters the Lord because he's standing under the knot. Some of the fluorescent green ink drips off the knot and runs down the Lord's face. The

English Lord lets the knot go and it stays hovering above his head, while he is standing under it. Standing under = understanding.

When you watch your mental movie, you'll see the Roman driving along in his chariot (the book of Romans) when he turns on the music and starts to jive (chapter five). As he's dancing he hits his gun and it fires with a loud 'bang!' (verse 1...) The bullet makes a huge hole in his shoe (verse ...2).

When you replay this story as a mental movie, you'll see the pro herbs with their sponsor's logos and advertising on their leaves (Proverbs), which are all disturbed by a large tree (chapter three) crashing down on them. Superman – our hero (verse 0...) – appears and picks up the tree, and starts to do the jive (verse ...5). Then the tree is thrown to the ground and trussed (trust) with a long rope. An English Lord (Lord) unties the tree using an awl (all), and the tree's cobweb covered heart from the time of yore (yore heart) bursts from its chest. The tree leans over the English Lord with a giant knot (lean not) which he then gives to the Lord to make his own (own). There's a violent storm but the Lord finds shelter by standing under (understanding) the giant knot.

You have now recalled:

Proverbs 3:05 "Trust __ ___ Lord ____ all your heart ___ lean not __ ____ own understanding".

Add the remaining filler words and without too much effort you have memorized Proverbs 3:5 "Trust in the Lord with all your heart and lean not on your own understanding".

You can see that if you were asked to recite Proverbs 3:5, you'd be able to start the story by substituting the fixed images for the book name and the numbers, and that will prompt you for the rest of the story and verse. Pretty cool, right?

8 REVISION FREQUENCY

When I first started using these techniques I 'revised' daily because I was so astonished at how well my memory was holding onto the verses. I wasn't really revising – I was mentally pinching myself and checking to see if the memories were still there. And they were as clear as the water on a Caribbean beach.

You'll be amazed at the 'stickiness' of these memory methods too, but you'll still need to do a small amount of revision to ensure the Lord's word is adopted into your long term memory. Having planted a Bible verse in your memory, you'd like it to take root there permanently.

The great news is that you won't need to revise the Bible verses even close to daily. The experts say that on average you'll need to rehearse them in your mind five times to ensure they're in your long term memory.

The recommended intervals between review sessions are ten minutes after you've learnt the verse; and then after one day; after one week; after one month; and after three to six months.

Five reviews. Simply press play on your mental movie and make sure that you can still see each image clearly.

I'm sure you'll agree that's quite appealing compared to repeating a verse fifty times to get it into your memory in the first place!

If you've chosen to learn a verse, you'll naturally want to use it, either by quoting the verse out loud or contemplating it in your mind. That's effective revision. Doing that, you'll soon be carrying the Lord's word permanently in your memory as well as in your heart.

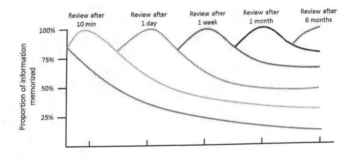

9 WHAT ALTERNATIVE METHODS ARE THERE?

The method taught in this book is easy to understand and use.

When we were putting together the Memory Audios™ for MemorizeBibleScripture.com we wanted to make them as simple as possible for our customers to use. We adapted other common memory techniques so that someone listening to a Memory Audio™ for the first time wouldn't need to learn a technique or system, they could just start listening and memorizing.

And that is the method you've learnt in this book.

However, there are other techniques commonly used by memory experts that you might like to explore and test for yourself. As you will see, they're also based on visualization and association.

We'll look at the Memory Palace method and also the Major System, and then discuss their strengths and weaknesses.

Memory Palace

Perhaps the oldest memory technique is called the *Memory Palace* or *Loci* method.

Think of a regular walk or journey you make that you can easily visualize. It might be from the front door of your home or building and through each of the rooms. Choose some particular locations along that journey.

The first one might be at the doormat outside your front door; the next just inside your front door; then as you walk through your home you pass the kitchen; and your bedroom door.

Now imagine for a moment that you've selected a Bible verse to memorize, chosen the key words and thought of some great substitute images.

Take one substitute image at a time and visualize it at a location on your mental walk through your home.

We'll use the start of Proverbs 3:5 again as an example.

Location	Substitute image
Doormat at front door	Trussed English Lord
Hallway inside front door	awl (leatherwork tool)
Middle of kitchen floor	cobweb covered heart
Bedroom door	leaning knot
...	...

Lying on the doormat at your front door is an English Lord who is completely trussed in a long continuous length of rope. As you step over him, open the door and walk inside, you see a giant awl – a leatherwork tool that looks like a sharp screwdriver or icepick – standing with its sharp end point upwards where the umbrella usually is. As you pass through your home and into the kitchen, you see on the floor a beating heart the size of a basketball and it's covered in cobwebs (from the time of yore). You continue walking and get to your bedroom door where you find a giant knot of rope leaning against the door and preventing you from entering.

From your short walk through your home, you have the start of Proverbs 3:5 **"Trust** in the **Lord** with **all your heart** and **lean not** ..."**

You can see how the 'Memory Palace' method links each substitute image with a fixed location on your walk through your home. This differs from the story method taught in this book which links each substitute image with the image that follows.

These differences create strengths and drawbacks that you can weigh up for yourself.

Strengths

- If you aren't able to recall a particular image, you can move on to the next location in your mind and you'll only miss one key word. The other key words will hopefully prompt you to recall what it is.

- It doesn't require a story linking each image, making it potentially quicker than the story method to implement.

Drawbacks

- Some work needs to be done before you can reliably use your Memory Palace. The order of your mental journey needs to be completely fixed. If you get some of the locations out of order you will mix up the order of your substitute images.

- You'll need to think of multiple journeys or Memory Palaces to use. You will be able to use a single mental journey for more than one verse – you'll be surprised how your mind will somehow file the verses separately – but soon you'll need more. This will limit how many verses you can memorize using this method.

Major System

Another common system used by memory experts is called the *Major* or *Phonetic* system.

Just as the Memory Palace gives you a fixed list of sequential locations to associate with memories – e.g. doormat, hallway, kitchen and bedroom – the Major System also provides a sequential list of fixed items to associate with memories.

Instead of locations on a journey, the Major System uses numbers – e.g. one, two, three and four. The purpose of this system is to transform that list of numbers into images that can be visualized. We then have a fixed image for each number, which we'll use in the same way as locations in the Memory Palace method.

Let's use the start of Proverbs 3:5 as an example again, and then I'll explain where the images for each number – known as 'pegs' – come from.

'Peg' word	Substitute image
One = Tie	Trussed English Lord
Two = Noah	awl (leatherwork tool)
Three = Ma	cobweb covered heart
Four = Rye	leaning knot
...	...

Your first image will always be associated with 'tie'. Imagine a brightly colored neck tie hanging in your wardrobe, and dangling on the end of the tie is an English Lord trussed up with a long piece of rope.

Your second image will always be associated with 'Noah'. Picture Noah walking along the deck of the ark. He's using a giant awl (leatherwork tool that looks like a sharp screwdriver or icepick) as a walking stick. The sharp end of the awl leaves holes in the timber deck when Noah leans on it.

The third image will always be associated with an image of 'Ma'. Your Ma is carrying a large jelly-like heart in her hands, and its rubbery sides are drooping towards the floor. The heart is completely covered in cobwebs, indicating it's from the time of yore.

'Rye' is the association for your fourth image. Visualize a huge slice of rye bread that is standing up on its edge. A length of rope which has an enormous knot tied in one end of it, walks up to the rye bread and leans against it. The rye bread grunts with the effort of staying upright against the weight of the leaning knot.

As you run through the 'peg' words in your mind, you'll be prompted with the associated images that will once again give you the start of Proverbs 3:5

"**Trust** in the **Lord** with **all your heart** and **lean not** …"

So where do the peg words or images come from?

There's a straightforward code that translates numbers into phonetic sounds.

Number	Phonetic sound
0	S or Z
1	T or D
2	N
3	M
4	R
5	L
6	Sh or Ch
7	K or G
8	F or V
9	P or B

To use larger numbers with more than one digit, you join the associated phonetic sounds together. So 43 becomes RM; 25 is NL; and 92 is PN. To turn those consonant sounds into meaningful words, you insert vowels, which have no related number values.

43 might become RaM; 25 could be NaiL; and 92 might be PeN. You then have an associated image for each number. By keeping that number/image combination fixed, you'll have a list of pegs in the same way that you have locations in your Memory Palace journey.

There are commonly used lists of peg words from 1-100 (search the internet and you'll find one easily) which can be learned and used straight away

You can see that the Major System is used in a similar way to the Memory Palace method. Each substitute image we're trying to memorize is associated with a known peg or location. And again, these methods rely on visualization and association.

Remember the rhyming words you learnt to memorize chapter and verse references? That's a great system because it's so easy to learn. When you're feeling comfortable with all of these new techniques, you could try using the Major System to memorize references instead of rhyming words.

Why would you want to do that? Instead of having three or four images to visualize and remember the chapter and verse reference, you could use just one or two images.

For example, if the chapter and verse was 9:10, our rhyming system would tell us to create a story using 'wine, gun and hero'. If we used the Major System, we could remember the reference with a single image of 'bats'. Decoding 'BaTS' to numbers gives us 910. That's a nice shortcut.

Like all memory systems, the Major System has strengths and drawbacks to be considered.

Strengths

- If you aren't able to recall a particular image, you can move on to the next 'peg' in your mind and you'll only miss one key word. The other key words will hopefully prompt you to recall what it is.

- It doesn't require a story linking each image, making it potentially quicker than the story method to implement.

- Unlike the Memory Palace method, if you don't recall a peg image (or location) you will be able to figure it out. For example, if you can't recall the peg word for 22 you will know that it is N_N. By running through the vowels to fill the blank space, you'll be reminded of the correct word. In my peg system 22 is 'nun'.

- The Major System allows you to jump straight to a number in your memorized list, although this benefit doesn't have much application for memorizing Bible verses. If you had memorized the Periodic Table of chemical elements and wanted to know the 17th element, you would jump straight to your mental peg for 17 of 'dog' and check your associated image. That's a lot quicker than running through the list from the beginning until you reach the 17th element.

Drawbacks

- The Major System requires the most preparation work of the methods we've looked at before you can begin using it to memorize Bible verses. Since the longest verse you'll memorize might have 30 or 40 key words, you need to have a fixed list of that many pegs ready to use.

- You will only be able to use one fixed list of pegs. This would be like having only one Memory Palace journey to use, and is limiting if you want to memorize many Bible verses. Having more than one peg word for each number will confuse you.

Your personal preference will decide which method you find most appropriate to use. The important thing to note is how each of these methods relies on visualization and association to tune into your memory.

10 SUMMARY

And there you have it, the know-how to memorize Bible verses without rote learning and repetition.

When I first learnt these expert memory techniques, I was filled with an amazing exhilaration. It was like someone had given me a super power, I was stunned by what my memory could do. Everyone who I've ever taught these methods to gets equally excited and I know you'll have that same feeling.

The secret to unlocking the amazing ability of your memory is visualization and association, not repeating something fifty times in a row. Thank goodness for that.

To quickly summarize the method you've just learned, there are three simple steps.

The *first* step is to select key words from the verse you'd like to memorize. With a bit of practice you'll figure out how many words in a verse you really need to recall before you can successfully remember the entire verse.

The *second* stage is to substitute key words and numbers for images. This includes the book, chapter and verse reference.

The rhyming word system we learnt for remembering numbers is one of the easiest methods. If you want to get even more efficient at memorizing references, consider using the Major System.

Finding substitute images for key words can be an interesting analysis of the English language and the way your mind works. What do you immediately picture in your mind when you see or hear a particular word?

The *third* and final step is to get creative and write some crazy stories to link your key images. The right side of your brain is going to be your closest ally in this stage. The more exaggerated and wild you make these stories, the easier it will be for your memory to grab and hold onto them.

While memorizing Bible verses has been the focus of this book, it isn't really the end goal. I hope that we've taught you how to learn scripture faster and easier than you ever thought possible, and that it gives you the freedom to focus on what's truly essential.

In my mind, the important part of the Lord's word is what you do with it in your daily life. That's when the journey really begins, and I wish you all the best on your Christian travels.

AUTHORS' NOTE

For those of you who are eager to memorize Bible verses as quickly as possible, please check out *"Memorize Bible Verses"* or visit www.MemorizeBibleScripture.com

We've done all of the work for you. After countless hours we have produced complete memory stories for 100 popular Bible verses.

You can choose the eBook or paperback editions or even try the audiobook format and discover what it's like to literally learn with your eyes closed!

The complete visual memory stories describe exactly what you need to visualize for each verse. You really can just lie back in bed or on the bus, close your eyes and picture in your mind each image and story. Your amazing memory will do the rest and you'll be able to recall the Lord's word whenever you like.

It's so exciting for us to help Christians everywhere learn scripture, and we hope you'll be able to carry the Lord's word with you every day in your mind as well as in your heart.

Best wishes,

Kyle and Dean

BONUS CHAPTER

The book *"Memorize Bible Verses: Complete Memory Stories for 100 Popular Verses"* almost places Bible verses into your memory for you. It tells you precisely what to visualize in your mind to remember the key words from some of the most popular verses in the Bible.

In this bonus chapter are five of those complete memory stories. Create a clear mental picture of everything described and let your amazing visual memory do the rest.

All verses are taken from the New International Version (NIV) Bible.

Ephesians 2:08

For it is by **grace you** have been **saved, through faith** –
and this is **not** from **yourselves,** it is the **gift** of **God** –

Reference story

A man is dressed as a large capital E, and despite his
costume he is freezing. He's an **_E freezing_**, covered in
icicles and shivering from cold. The E tries to put a large
woolen **_shoe_** onto his foot to keep it warm, but there's
something in the shoe. He pulls it out and discovers it's a
doll of Superman (our **_hero_**). The E is very annoyed at this
and throws the doll away. It hits your front **_gate_** (or any
gate you can picture clearly) and somehow sticks to the
gate, maybe because the doll is covered in slime.

E freezing, shoe, hero, gate = Ephesians 2:08

Keywords: For __ __ __ grace you ____ ____ saved,
through faith – ___ ____ __ not ____ yourselves, __ __
___ gift __ God –

The Superman doll slowly slides down the gate, leaving a
trail of slime behind him. When he eventually falls on the
ground, he lands on a number **_four_**. The number four is
like a stuffed toy, but instead of being an animal, it's a
number four, with arms and legs.
FOUR = FOR.

The four picks up the Superman doll and decides it looks
very tasty. The four is thankful for this little snack that has
fallen into its lap, and so it says **_grace_** "For what we're
about to receive, may the Lord make us truly thankful".
GRACE.

Just as the four is about to eat the Superman, a **_ewe_**

appears next to the four. A ewe is a female sheep and you know she is female because she is wearing a long dress and high heeled shoes.

EWE = YOU.

She reaches out and saves Superman just as he was about to be devoured by the hungry four. **_Saved_** him just in time.

A DRAMATIC RESCUE = SAVED.

To make sure the Superman is really out of the clutches of the hungry four, the ewe throws him. He flies through the air and right **_through Faith_** Hill, the American country singer and celebrity.

THROUGH FAITH HILL = THROUGH FAITH.

Faith Hill doesn't realize Superman has gone right through her, and looks down at her stomach. She sees a large **_knot_** of string sticking out.

KNOT = NOT.

She pulls one end of the string and out of her stomach tumble some cobweb-covered elves. They're covered in cobwebs because they are from the time of yore, meaning they are very old.

YORE ELVES = YOURSELVES.

The elves are carrying a brightly wrapped **_gift_**, with a large bow on top.

GIFT.

The elves unwrap the gift and out pops an old white haired man, who looks just like the depiction of God from Michelangelo's Sistine Chapel. He represents **_God_**.

GIFT OF GOD.

John 1:12

Yet to all **who** did **receive him,** to those **who believed** in his **name,** he **gave** the **right** to **become children** of **God**

Reference story

John Lennon is walking along the street when a large **gun** jumps out of nowhere and tries to rob him. (John Lennon was one of the Beatles. If you don't know what he looks like, either Google an image of him or use another John whom you can easily visualize - John Travolta, John F Kennedy, or a friend or relative named John). This gun has arms and legs and is the size of a person. John Lennon falls to the ground, does a commando roll to the side, and pulls out his own **gun** from his shoulder holster in one fluid movement. It's very reminiscent of Bruce Willis or Matt Damon in an action movie. John Lennon fires off a quick snap shot at the huge gun, but that's where his smooth moves end, because he unfortunately manages to shoot himself in the **shoe**. It is a very large shoe and the bullet goes through the toe of the shoe without hitting his foot.

John Lennon, gun, gun, shoe = John 1:12

Keywords: Yet __ ___ who ___ receive him, __ _____ who believed __ ___ name, __ gave ___ right __ become children __ God –

After going through his shoe, the bullet misses the other gun and goes through a nearby wall. There is a howl of pain from the other side of the wall, and out jumps a full sized **yeti**, leaping around and rubbing his belly. The yeti is about 7 feet tall and covered in long shaggy hair all over its body.

YETI = YET.

As it is jumping around it bumps into an owl. This owl is the size of a chair, with a really fat body but tiny small wings. It was just sitting there, quietly saying '***hoo***, hoo, hoo' to itself when it gets body slammed out of nowhere by the yeti bouncing around, yelping in pain. The owl gives out a prolonged 'hoooooo' like a slowly deflating balloon and lies on the ground.

OWL SAYING 'HOO' = WHO.

A group of choirboys appears and starts to sing the owl a hymn, like they're giving him a gift. So the owl continues to lie there and ***receives the hymn***.

RECEIVES HYMN = RECEIVE HIM.

Then another owl swoops in. This ***owl*** is tiny in comparison to the chair-sized owl on the floor, but he looks very strong.

OWL = HOO = WHO.

The tiny owl is carrying a big bag, which he opens and empties on the large owl. The bag is full of leaves, but they're all yellow and black and in the shape of bees. They're bee leaves. Now the large owl has been covered in leaves, he's been ***bee leaved***.

BEE LEAVED = BELIEVED.

The leaves completely cover the large owl except for a small spot on his chest where his ***nametag*** shows through. Make his name whatever you like (I'm going to choose 'Hoo' – Hoo the owl), but focus on picturing the nametag.

NAMETAG = NAME.

Everyone is acting like Hoo had died, but suddenly he leaps up, shaking bee leaves off himself. He **_gives_** the small owl a notebook that has a **_right_** hand attached to it. It is **_writing_**.

GIVES THE RIGHT HAND WRITING = GAVE THE RIGHT.

The small owl is very touched and in return gives the large owl a **_comb_** in the shape of a **_bee_** to comb his feathers.

BEE COMB = BECOME.

The large owl starts to preen and comb himself with the bee comb. Then a noisy group of **_children_** come running up, all excited to see such a large owl and trying to pat him. Chasing them and trying to get them to calm down is an old white haired man, who looks like Michelangelo's depiction of God from the Sistine Chapel. He represents **_God_**, and the children are his.

CHILDREN WITH OLD WHITE HAIRED MAN = CHILDREN OF GOD.

Matthew 6:33

But seek first his **kingdom** and his **righteousness,** and **all** these **things will** be **given** to **you** as **well.**

Reference story

You go to wipe your feet on a door**mat**, but there are some sticks sticking up in the mat, which you don't see. When you try to wipe your feet, the ***sticks*** poke right into one of your feet. Ouch. You turn to run away from the mat and run face first into a large ***tree***. Thump. You fall backwards and lie looking up at the sky with your injured face and foot. Above you, you watch a small thin tree growing up very close to you, the branches and leaves extending and growing as you watch. And then you realize it is the stick that is still in your foot which has started to grow into a ***tree***.

Mat, sticks, tree, tree = Matthew 6:33

Keywords: But seek first ___ kingdom ___ ___ righteousness, ___ all _____ things will __ given __ you __ well.

The thin tree abruptly leans over and starts to use one of its thin branches to whip your ***butt***. Your butt is being covered in large red welts, while you are still lying on the ground.
BUTT = BUT.

You try and get away. You bounce around on your butt trying to get away from the tree, but it's difficult since the tree has you pinned by the foot. You eventually rip your foot away from the tree and run away, but the tree chases you and it turns into a game of hide and ***seek***. The tree is relentlessly seeking you, like in a bad dream. You hide in

one spot but the tree seeks you out and forces you to find another place to hide.
SEEK.

You're running as fast as you can to get away from the tree and you overtake some runners on a running track. You burst through the finishing line at the end of the track and take **_first_** place, for which you're awarded a medal and blue ribbon - first.
WINNER'S MEDAL = FIRST.

You're standing on a podium where you are awarded first place, and then strangely you are also presented with a crown and created king. You look out and can see your new **_kingdom_**, with a castle and vast lands of rolling green hills. Your kingdom is beautiful.
KINGDOM.

Then your kingdom turns into a giant chessboard made of black and white squares. Your subjects are lined up on the chessboard dressed as pawns, knights and bishops, and they are all writing furiously. They barely look up as they write letters, books, and essays. It's a giant game of **_write chess_**. And in the middle of the board you can see **_Ness_** the Loch Ness Monster wondering casually through the black and white squares.
WRITE CHESS NESS = RIGHTEOUSNESS.

And then all of the chess pieces stop their writing and start to battle each other. Each of them is armed with an awl. An **_awl_** is a leatherwork tool, and looks like an ice pick or a sharp screwdriver, but these are giant awls and are the size of swords.
AWL = ALL.

It's a frightening battle with each chess piece swinging their awl furiously. Then a giant Thing falls out of the sky

to stop the fighting. The Thing is the Marvel Comic character from the Fantastic Four stories, who like he's made from bright orange rocks and is about eight feet tall. Then another giant Thing falls out of the sky, then another – now there are three ***Things.***
COMIC BOOK HERO 'THING' = THINGS.

The Things stop the chess pieces fighting momentarily and start reading out everyone's will and testament, one by one, in case are killed in the fighting. Each **_will_** is a long scroll of paper like a roll of toilet paper.
WILL.

After reading the will for each chess piece, the Things are ***given two ewes*** by the chess pieces. A ewe is a female sheep, and you can tell they're female because they're wearing a short pink striped dress.
GIVEN TWO EWES = GIVEN TO YOU.

Now the Things have two large ewes and they're not sure where to keep them, so they drop them down a water **_well_**, a deep hole in the ground filled with spring water. The ewes fall down the well and land with a giant splash in the water at the bottom.
WELL.

Galatians 5:22

But the **fruit** of the **Spirit** is **love, joy, peace, patience, kindness, goodness, faithfulness**

Reference story

There is a bright yellow pair of **_galoshes_** (gumboots) sitting on the ground. Some music starts in the background and the toes of the galoshes start to tap the ground in time to the music. Then the music starts to pick up in tempo, and the galoshes get up and start to **_jive_** with each other, dancing and spinning. They bump into a high-heeled **_shoe_** as they're jiving away. The shoe looks like it is going to get angry and punch the galoshes but then a basketball **_shoe_** gets in between them and cools things down.

Galoshes, jive, shoe, shoe = Galatians 5:22

Keywords: But ____ fruit __ ____ Spirit __ love, joy, peace, patience, kindness, goodness, faithfulness

After the galoshes and high-heeled shoe have cooled down, the basketball shoe starts to back away. But it trips and falls flat on its **_butt_**. Imagine the thump it makes and see the basketball shoe rubbing its sore butt. Its butt is glowing red with pain and the shoe looks around for something to make it feel better.
BUTT = BUT.

There is a bowl of **_fruit_** nearby so the basketball shoe sits on top of the fruit in the hope some fruit therapy will ease the pain. There are mangos and bananas and strawberries and peaches. No pineapples, thankfully.
BOWL OF FRUIT = FRUIT.

As the basketball shoe is sitting on top of the fruit, a large white sheet floats down out of the sky and covers them all. They look like a lumpy Halloween **_spirit_**, dressed in a white sheet with holes for eyes.
SPIRIT COSTUME = SPIRIT.

The white sheet suddenly starts to heave and move around as something begins to happen beneath it. A gentle stream of **_love hearts_** begins to dribble out from its edges. There are hundreds of tiny pink glowing love hearts that pour onto the floor in a steady stream.
LOVE HEARTS = LOVE.

The love hearts flow onto the ground, creating a large pool of love hearts. A woman is walking along and slips in the pool of love hearts and falls over. When the woman gets up, she is smiling, happy and obviously filled with **_joy_**. And by coincidence her name is **_Joy_** (if you happen to know someone named Joy then picture them), and she is singing the hymn **_Joy_** to the World.
JOY, SINGING JOY AND FILLED WITH JOY = JOY.

Joy straightens her dress and flashes the **_peace sign_**. She does that by extending her index and middle finger with the other fingers closed and the palm of her hand facing outward. Her index finger and middle finger are unusually long, three times as long as her other fingers. Her peace sign is very dramatic, to say the least.
PEACE SIGN = PEACE.

As she is walking along flashing the peace sign, Joy walks past a hospital. All of the **_patients_** start giving her the peace sign in return. There are hundreds of patients, dressed in pale blue gowns, some of them walking, some of them lying on beds, some of them with their gowns gaping open at the back, and all of them giving Joy the

peace sign.
HOSPITAL PATIENTS = PATIENCE.

Then the patients all start to slowly walk out of the hospital and try to cross the road. But the road is very busy with lots of traffic and most of the patients aren't able to walk very well. So, helping them across the intersection is the Loch Ness monster, named **_Ness_**. Picture her as a cross between a dragon and a lizard. Ness is being incredibly **_kind_** to all of the patients, making sure they're feeling alright, helping them to walk, holding up the traffic to make sure they get across the road safely, and speaking to them with an incredibly kind voice.
NESS BEING VERY KIND = KINDNESS.

Once Ness has kindly helped all of the patients across the road, they all turn and each of them gives **_Ness_** a **_gold star_**. They are to go on her forehead for **_being so good_**, like a little child in first grade in primary school who has been good. Because there are so many gold stars given to Ness she ends up with her forehead completely plastered in gold stars, so she must have been extremely good.
NESS WITH GOLD STARS FOR BEING GOOD = GOODNESS.

Ness is very proud of herself. All of the patients have successfully crossed the road. Unfortunately, the traffic has been held up a little bit and some of the drivers are annoyed at the delay and honk their horns at Ness. Ness grabs one of the drivers and pulls her out of her car. She is a blond lady and you realize it's **_Faith Hill_**, the American country singer and celebrity. In a surprise move, Ness swallows Faith in one big mouthful and gulp. **_Ness_** then has a very bad belly ache because she's **_full of Faith_**.
NESS FULL OF FAITH HILL = FAITHFULNESS.

Romans 6:23

For the **wages** of **sin** is **death, but** the **gift** of **God** is **eternal life** in **Christ Jesus** our **Lord.**

Reference story

There are two **_Roman_** soldiers dressed up in their armor and they decide to have a fight. They don't want to hurt each other too much, so they decide to use **_sticks_**. The first soldier picks up a small stick and gets ready to do battle, but then the second soldier picks up a branch. The first soldier gets a bit scared and pulls off a **_shoe_** and throws it at his opponent. It bounces off harmlessly, so the first soldier grabs a **_tree_** and tries to uproot it and use it against the other soldier's branch.

Romans, sticks, shoe, tree = Romans 6:23

Keywords: For ___ wages __ sin __ death, but ___ gift __ God __ eternal life __ Christ Jesus ___ Lord.

As the soldier tries to swing the tree, it turns into a giant **_four-leaf clover_**, and waves harmlessly past his opponent. **FOUR LEAF CLOVER = FOUR = FOR.**

As he swings the four-leaf clover, an envelope marked '**_wages_**' drops out of his pocket. It's his pay packet, filled with **_gold coins_**, which spill all over the ground. **GOLD COINS = WAGES.**

Both of the soldiers pick up the wages/money and go and spend it all on food. They proceed to eat all the food, becoming **_gluttons_**. They eat a huge pile of food and grow fat, very **_sinful_**. **GLUTTONY = SIN.**

One of them eats so much his stomach bursts at the seams, and he dies. What a grisly *death*!
DEATH.

The other soldier can't bear to look at the face of his dead colleague and turns him over so his huge fat ***butt*** is pointing to the sky. The butt is now enormous and looks like a small mountain.
BUTT = BUT.

From out of the sky falls a gift and it lands with a 'thud' right on the dead man's butt. The rolls of fat on the butt wobble with the impact. The ***gift*** is brightly wrapped with an enormous bow.
GIFT.

Out of the gift jumps an old man with long white hair. He looks just like Michelangelo's depiction of God on the Sistine Chapel, and has white hair and flowing robes. He represents ***God***.
GOD.

The old man jumps into a car and does an E turn. Not a U turn, but an ***E turn***. There's a lot of reversing and turning involved as the car outlines the letter E.
E TURN = ETERNAL.

As the car moves away there is the sound of hundreds of eggs cracking. Suddenly there are hundreds of small fluffy yellow ***chicks*** (baby chickens) piling up in the car and falling out the windows. The new-born chicks represent *life*.
BABY CHICKS = LIFE.

The car is driving along with the chicks falling out the windows when it runs into ***Jesus***. He has long dark hair and a beard and is wearing flowing white clothes, but on

the front of his white robe is a large, neon green **_cross_**. The cross blinks on and off, making it very eye catching.
CROSS JESUS = CHRIST JESUS.

The car quickly reverses to get away from this cross Jesus and there's a thud as it reverses over something. Underneath the car now is an **_English Lord_**. The Lord is wearing a long white wig and a red gown with white fur lining. His wig isn't so white now since he's lying on the ground and he is leaking a bit of blood.
ENGLISH LORD = LORD.

ABOUT THE AUTHORS

Kyle Buchanan and Dean Roller are the founding directors of Memory Worldwide Pty Ltd, a company specializing in memory training and the innovation of educational products.

They co-authored *"How to Memorize Bible Verses: The Fast and Easy Way to Memorizing Scripture"*, which quickly became the #1 best-selling book in Christian Education on Amazon.com. Their latest venture is MemorizeBibleScripture.com, helping Christians memorize scripture in the most effective way.

With six university degrees between them, Kyle and Dean understand the process of research and learning. Their latest research focus is in the fields of educational and cognitive psychology as they study and write about memory mnemonic techniques and their practical application.

Kyle and Dean's goal is to help you learn and memorize new information faster and easier than you ever imagined was possible.

To learn more about scripture memorization, visit www.MemorizeBibleScripture.com

26751787R10047

Made in the USA
Lexington, KY
14 October 2013